1920's BOY — Recollection of a Yorkshire Childhood

STANLEY R. BOARDMAN

1973

Designed and produced by The Ridings Publishing Company, Driffield, Yorkshire and printed by their associate company, Halstead Print and Publications, Station Approach, Driffield, Yorkshire

Telephone: (037 72) 3232

About the Author

STANLEY BOARDMAN opted out of the 'rat race'
of living for 12 months to work (as a signwriter)
when he felt like it (or needed the cash) and
to spend the rest of his time putting on canvas his
thoughts, feelings, experiences as a boy in the 1920's.

Stanley Boardman is a self-taught artist and claims
his 'education' has been from the world around him ...
"from numerous Public Libraries, innumerable
Public Houses, the Great British Army,
the street, market places, shops, garages, fairgrounds,
gypsy encampments etc. etc."

This book reproduces (in miniature form) the pictures
that resulted from his 'year off', and show the
contrasting moods of poverty and high spirits, drabness
and colour of his boyhood.

Stanley Boardman

HOW IT ALL STARTED

LET ME first give you a bit of "gen" how this "1920's Boy" lark came about, eh?

Our Jo (that's my missis) was "fed up." She'd had enough of a being shopkeeper and wanted to be "an ordinary housewife like other women" she announced.

Our Jill, that's our youngest daughter, was fed up too. She said: "There's no home life here!" (she's a big believer in "home life") ."It's like living in ruddy Woolworth's; there's Toys in the toilet and bikes in the bedrooms . . . it's 'orrible!"

Our Marian, the eldest daughter (she's the practical one) never liked it right from the start. She'd got herself wed and blown.

The rot really set in when one morning I opened the box my electric shaver lived in and there on top was the first of our Jill's Brainwashing Campaign.

Very simple, very neat, no messing about, straight to the point, a piece of paper bearing the message:

> SELL THE SHOP

I went to sit on the throne to ponder this, and there behind the lavatory door:

> SELL THE SHOP

The Boardman Kids . . . 1920's children

I served the first customer that morning, one of the kids on his way to school. A two bob Airfix kit.

He gave me half a crown.

I went to the till to get him his tanner change.

Opened the drawer.

KAPOW!

She'd stuck again.

SELL THE SHOP

We decided to look for a house.

It had to have some sort of outbuilding with it for me to do my Signwriting in.

We found it. A big, beautiful, detached old house, complete with a barn, at Steeton, the next village, a mile or so up the road.

Asked the man how much he wanted for it.

That settled the price we had to get for the shop, known far and wide as "The Paint Box", Kirkgate, Silsden, run by them "balmy Boardmans."

Janet Lampkin, (famous sister of them three brothers that mess about with motor-bikes) went to see her old man.

The deal was done. Janet had the "Paint Box," Silsden.

Our Mum, Our Jill and me had "Sunny Bank," Steeton. We were skint again.

Two or three years later along comes Steve, sweeps our Jilly off her feet, and before you could say "Sell the shop" wedding bells are ringing for him and our gal.

Our Jo and me were on our tod.

"Right then, this is it!" we said, "Rat-race, you've had it!"

The house was paid for, Jo fixed herself up with a part-time job at the hospital and loves every minutes of it. We decided that if we lived a very simple homely life, no holidays, no cars, no fancy clobber, none of the unnecessary, expensive material things of life, we could manage nicely if I only worked two or three days a week Signwriting — plus my Army Pension.

The rest of the time Jo could potter in her beloved garden and greenhouse (I built this for her out of reject window frames from a local building manufacturers, the whole kaboodle only cost about ten quid).

I could look after Puscus the Moggy, (we didn't really care much for moggies at first, but found we had to have one, the barn was wick with meeces, and while I prefer meeces to moggies, our Jo's scared bowlegged of the "dirty little beasts"). A couple of dozen hens and bantams in the hen-run at the back of the house, and do just what the 'ell we like — in my case, painting pictures.

WE'D BEEN out to supper one night at Pam and Ken Boulton's in Silsden.

Pam had just resigned after umpteen years as a school teacher. She'd had enough. It wasn't like it used to be. Didn't like it any more.

We got talking about the sort of life kids live to-day. Jo and I told them what it was like when we were kids in the 1920's.

They were spellbound. They'd never realised how poverty-stricken every thing was then.

"You ought to write a book about it!" said Pam.

"Write!" sez I, "Hell, it takes me all my time to talk English never mind write it!" (No education you know old boy, dead rough, common as muck like.)

"No!" she says, "that's true, but you can paint, why don't you paint it?"

So I did. Solid, for the next eighteen months.

My auditor said: "What's happened to the business, you've had a shocking year?"

"That's where you're wrong mate!" says I, "I've had the best year I've ever had!"

He didn't understand.

I didn't care.

"1920's Boy" had come to life.

EX-SERVICEMEN

MY OLD lady told me that as she walked about during the night feeding me, she could hear the drone of the German Zeppelin Airships on their way to bomb London.

The place . . . Maidstone, Kent.

The time: during the first World War.

By the time I was old enough to look around and sort things out a bit for myself, scenes like these were all too familiar all over the country.

"*Your Country Needs You !*" the posters read.

"*Enlist To-day !*"

"*Fight For A Country Fit For Heroes To Live In !*"

The young men had gone in their thousands.

The reluctant ones and the frightened ones had been persuaded to go by being handed white feathers (the mark of cowardice) in the streets.

It takes less courage to face the chatter of enemy machine guns than the scorn of one's womenfolk.

The really brave ones stuck to their pacifist guns, were called "conchies" (Conscientious Objectors) and were thrown into jail.

I wonder how those who had handed out the white feathers felt as they dished out their coppers to the by now armless, legless, sightless, and even worse, hopeless "heroes"?

But this is all a long time ago; there have been other wars since then.

We have very short memories.

THE SPIKE — THE GRUBBER
or to give it its official title
THE WORKHOUSE

I SUPPOSE it's a matter of comparison really . . . after seeing this huddled, muddled, down-and-out queue of human misery every evening on our way home from school, waiting for the "Workhouse Master" to unlock those forbidding-looking iron gates, to let them in for a night's doss, knowing full well they'd be turfed out of town the following day, to face another ten or twelve miles trudge to the next town and the next workhouse, regardless of the weather, face another ten or twelve miles trudge to the next town their health or their age.

Homeless, penniless, tired out, hungry and unwanted.

I could never make up my mind as to whether the high stone walls, the iron railings and the locked gates were designed to keep the poor souls in or to keep them out.

To be able to go home to our little terrace house with its welcoming gas-light, its stone-flagged floors, coconut matting and tab-rugs, to a king-size hunk of bread and jam in front of a merrily-blazing coal fire . . . one felt like a millionaire.

I suppose it's all a matter of comparison really.

THE COTTAGE HOME

THESE weren't bad kids.

They weren't juvenile delinquents as they are called to-day.

Most of them weren't even orphans.

They just had the misfortune to be born at the wrong time.

Their parents were unable to keep a roof over their heads, so they finished up in the "Cottage Home."

Some of them came to Holycroft School with us, we called them "Kotti-jomers."

I used to feel most sorry for them on beautiful summer evenings. We would be having a 'ell of a time in Holme House Woods, swimming naked in the dam belonging to Stell's Tube Mills, paddling in the beck, climbing trees, or sliding down the stony banks on our britches behinds, making it necessary later to put patches on the patches.

They would be marched through the woods, two by two, with their close-cropped heads, coarse grey "workhouse" suits, and their big army-style boots always — it seemed to me — with the laces undone.

One little lad in particular really used to make me feel sad. Thin and forlorn looking, he used to turn round and envy us our freedom, with big appealing brown eyes.

I wanted to show him in my picture, but I thought it might embarrass him; he still lives in Keighley. Also, I thought you might think I was overdoing the "sob-stuff."

You see, Mick, (that's not his real name) only had one leg. I never liked to ask him what happened to the other one. In its place was a wooden peg.

Whenever I see him now, he is very smartly dressed and seems to have done alright for himself.

You would never recognise him now from my description of him as a lad. We always pass a cheery word, but I don't know why. Neither of us have ever mentioned those earlier meetings, those many long years ago.

EMILY MATCHBOX

WHAT is fame? Ask anyone who lived in or around Keighley in the 1920's or 30's if they can remember the name of the town's Mayor, in any given year, or for that matter, who aws Prime Minister of England . . . I'm afraid you'll draw many blanks.

Ask the same people "Who was Emily Matchbox?" man-jack of them will be able to tell you.

Emily was one of Keighley's many "characters." A rag, a bone, and a hank of hair. Summer and winter she sang and danced in the streets and market-places of the old town, dressed in a tatty old coat, held together with "straw-band" for a belt, and safety pins for buttons. A pair of size ten men's boots, without laces, salvaged from some sleazy back street dustbin. Grey, (very grey) lisle stockings, more holey than godly, draped round her skinny legs.

This saying "more holey than Godly," derives from another old maxim "cleanliness is next to Godliness" originated no doubt by some splendid gent with a bathroom and hot running water. Where the only washing facilities, including clothes, for families of eight, nine or more, was a sandstone slab of a sink, two or three inches deep, under a cold-water tap, in a pint-size cellar-head kitchen, or even in a cupboard in the living-room, Godliness, I fear, often went out through the window.

Emily Matchbox didn't have a real home, or any money. She didn't really need either; there were plenty of disused "cellar-'oles" in the slum property all over the place to "kip" in. She was well-known by every shopkeeper and market trader in the district.

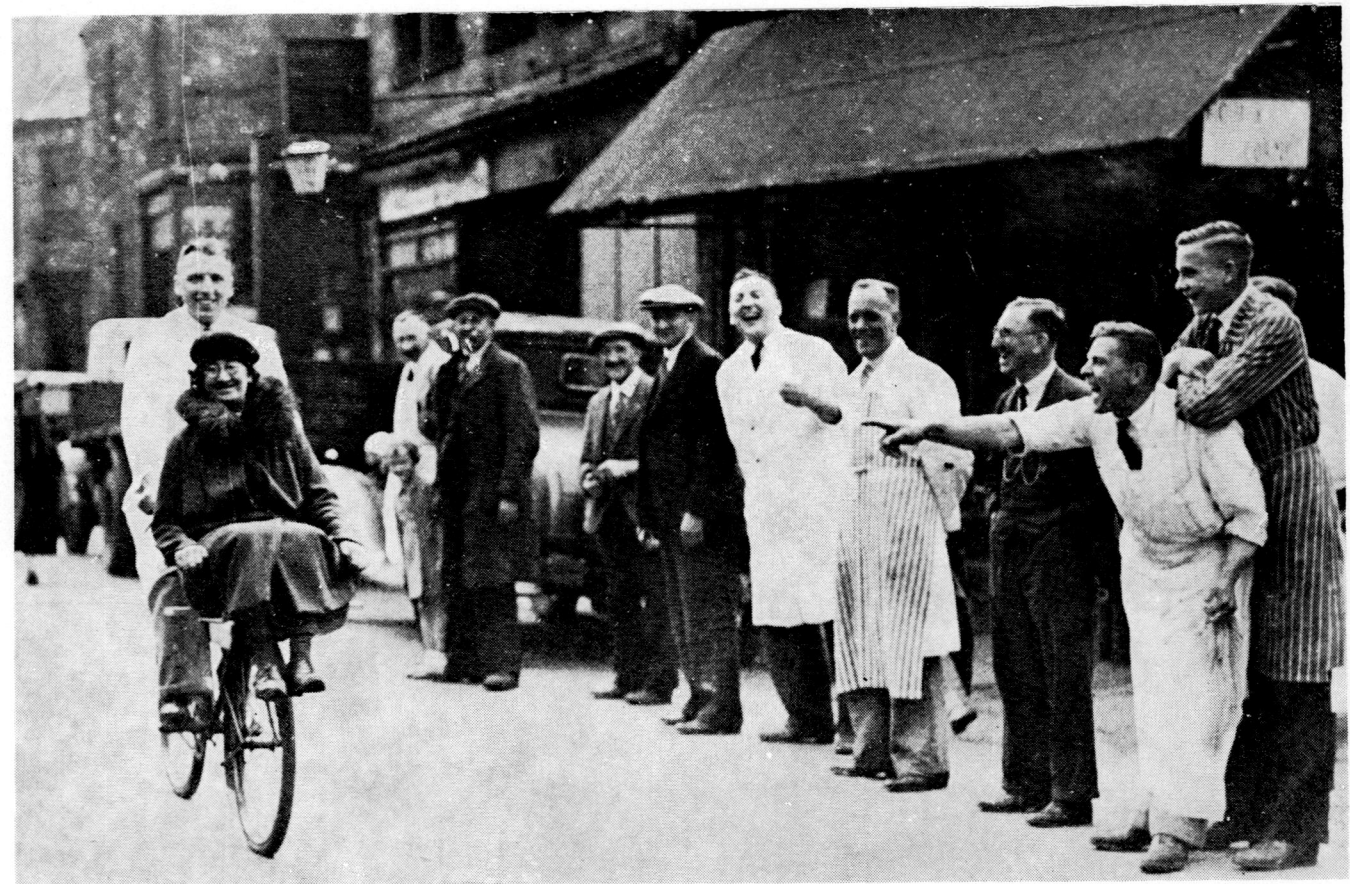

Her little "song and dance act," and her infectious laughter were ample payment for the odd stale loaf of bread, yesterday's pork pies, sausages, green-groceries, and so on.

She wanted for nothing.

In the early 1940's, the coldest, bleakest years of the war, our "wandering minstrel" was still mooching around with her croaky old songs, and by now, creaky old dance, cheering the wives and sweethearts of the departed shopkeepers who were away in the services, the Special Police, or the town's munition factories.

Our "middle" sister, Kathleen, a tall, graceful, brown-eyed girl, was manageress of a stationer's shop in North Street, doing a roaring trade in writing paper, envelopes, fountain pens, etc. Kath was one of Emily's favourites.

On cold, cheerless mornings, she would invite the shivering, dishevelled figure, straight from the dirty, freezing "cellar-'ole" of a home, into the bright warm back room of the shop, for a cup of hot chocolate, a few biscuits, a welcome warm by the fire, and many times a copper or two to see her on her way.

Came the day when Kath's boy-friend, "Jock," a Commando from one of the Scottish regiments, "popped the question." The wedding was fixed for his next leave at Fell Lane Chapel.

The story has it that Emily had been quite upset because she had nothing to give as a wedding present to her beloved young friend.

On the morning of the happy day, a smiling, radiant Kathleen and her smart new soldier husband came hand-in-hand from the chapel and stood at the top of the steps, receiving the congratulations of their many friends and neighbours.

Suddenly, from across the other side of the lane came a weird and wonderful sound.

All eyes turned.

There was our rag-bag of a heroine. She had got up early that morning to trudge the two long uphill miles from Keighley to deliver the only wedding present she could afford . . . The Emily Matchbox Song and dance act.

THE LAST MILE

CAP AND BULL

NOTHING I've ever seen at the "flicks," or on "telly," or anywhere else, has ever given me the kick we used to get out of this caper.

Kick, perhaps, is too mild a word. I'm not kidding, it used to ruddy well scare me bowlegged.

The rules of the game are quite simple, (I think we must have been, too). You take it in turns at throwing each other's cap at the bull. Then you've got to go and get it, (the cap, not the bull). That gets you if you don't head for that gate like the clappers.

I've seen blokes clear it without so much as touching the top, and land with a thud into the mud on the safe side, whilst a split second later the bull arrived with a bigger thud on the other.

Phew! — Thank the Lord my turn's over.

THE TINGERLAIRIE MAN

"WHERE the Blue Danube flows along"

"The Lily of Laguna"

"Roses of Picardy"

"It's a long way to Tipperary"

"Smile awhile"

All this and much, much more, all for a penny or a jam-jar, "Tank-a-you-a-werry much-a-sir!"

"Tank-a-you too Taony, it was lovely."

Note the bucket, when this was full it was worth one penny (real money) to a rose-grower I knew.

WASH DAY

UGH! — the lousiest day of the week.

Everywhere 's wet and steamy.

The house is miserable.

Everybody's bad-tempered.

Mum had to get up at six o'clock in the morning to light the fire under the red brick "copper" that stands across the corner of the kitchen.

Then she has to fill the boiler with cold water, a bucket full at a time.

She's got her blue and white polka dot mop cap on. Her greying hair straggles out from under it, all sweaty wet.

Her sleeves are rolled up her thin rough red arms, and she has her Tate and Lyle sugar-bag pinny on.

When the clothes have boiled for a bit, out they come on the end of a stick in to the Peggy-tub. They're possed with the posser and they're knocked 'ell out of on the rubbing-board.

It stinks of mucky clothes, and sweaty bodies and carbolic soap.

It doesn't pay to ask for a slice of bread and jam or a lump of parkin at this stage; Mum's south country accent and oaths are strongest at this point.

By the time we come home from school at dinner-time it's time to help with the Wringer.

The big old cast-iron mangle creaks and groans as we take it in turns at turning the big heavy wheel.

If it's raining there's wet clothes on clothes-horses and clothes lines hanging all over the place. Wet shirts and socks and nightgowns drape around your face as you come through the door.

It's lousy sheep's-head broth for dinner, "and think yourselves dam lucky to get that you ungrateful lot of perishers. If you aren't careful I'll have the whole miserable bunch of you in the dam Cottage Home!"

God! Let's get to 'ell out of here.

It's nearly a relief to be going back to school, but that's lousy too — I hate it!

Miserable, 'orrible, stinking Monday!

FIREWOOD RACING CARS
(with drawing pin wheels)

ANOTHER one of our favourite sayings . . . "If you've got no socks, you can't pull 'em up!"

But if you've got no toys and you want toys, but you ain't got no money, what's the answer? Make 'em yourself, of course!

So you get a piece of firewood, a penknife, some drawing pins, a tree stump to sit on, a little bit of imagination, and before you can say "Malcolm Campbell," not only do you have toys, you have a day at Le Mans thrown in for good measure.

DRESSED POULTRY

THEY taught young Jim to pluck newly-killed old hens.

Young Jim was mighty proud of this, so to demonstrate his new-found skill, he plucked two or three.

This caused one heck of a row: you see, these were not newly-killed old hens at all, they were very much alive young hens.

Even that might not have been too bad, but these very much alive young hens belonged to a very irate man in another pen, who made it quite clear to all and sundry, he liked his hens better as they were before, *"Dressed Poultry."*

BAND OF HOPE

WHAT a dedicated, patient, kindly lot of people those "Band of Hope" teachers must have been.

To put up with the antics of the scruffy, unruly bunch of "couldn't-care-less," pot of tea and currant-bun scrounging set of right villains that were us, they deserved a medal as big as a frying-pan.

"Band of Hopeless" would have been a far more apt title.

Not that they had all that much success with us in later life, either.

They got us all to sign *"The Pledge of Total Abstinence from all Intoxicating Liquor."*

We chanted: "My Drink is Water Bright" at the top of our 'orrible raucous voices, and as soon as me and my immediate buddies, at any rate, were old enough, every man-jack of us headed for the nearest boozer.

The closest we ever got to praying was during the war. Jerry was knocking 'ell out of us, right, left, and centre. Dirty great Stuka Dive-Bombers were diving, screeching, and throwing all sorts of 'orrible bombs and stuff at us in an attempt to stop us from scarpering a right bit sharpish back to Blighty via the channel ports.

Then we used to get down on our unworthy, knocky knees and say "Hell-fire, if there'a anybody up there besides them lousy Jerries, please, please, help us now!"

So, to the few of you that are still with us, (and I'm afraid there are only a few, now) I'd like to say a very belated "Thank You."

You didn't have all that much success with the religious, or the abstinence bits, but if I live to be a hundred, (and you never know, I might; my Grandad Boardy did just that), I shall be eternally grateful to you all for the kindness and tolerance you showed us.

THE SLAUGHTER HOUSE

FIRST, let me explain why we passed this horrible place so frequently.

We lived at the top of Fell Lane, a delightful village-like place of terraced cottages and small farmsteads.

Our "playgrounds" were Holme-House Woods, (little changed to this day), Branshaw Moors and quarries, Newsholme Dene, Bailey Park, and further on, miles and miles of beautiful wild moorlands, inhabited only by the grouse (shouting to us to "Go-back!" — "Go-back!"), the peewits, Curlews, Sparrow-Hawks and Kestrels.

There were lizards and frogs, dragon-flies and rabbits and hares, a veritable paradise for school-hating boys.

On past Slippery-Ford to the Big-Dam and Cowling Pinnacle. Our childhood was a delight of freedom, especially during the school's summer holidays, the happiest period of all. One whole month of discipline-free wandering and playing in all these glorious places.

But I digress . . . back to the slaughter-house.

To get to two very important places vital to our existence, we walked to the bottom of Fell Lane, down Oakworth Road, past the grim-looking, iron-railed and gated Workhouse, with many a fearful sidelong glance, dreading that we would ever finish up in there. Down to Damside in all its squalor and its fighting, squabbling residents. Across the broken-down-looking Quebec Bridge. Here we would stop and look over the parapet to watch, and throw stones at the rats ("as big as blinking moggies!") scuttling and scavenging amongst the filth and debris of the stinking, rubbish-filled North Beck.

Through the "ginnel-'ole" past an "edifice" that never ceased to fill us with awe, amazement and nausea.

Built out over the beck, and held up by iron supports, a three or four "stall" cast-iron Urinal. Its sides, back, front and ends were made of slabs of cast metal pierced with hundreds of half-inch holes in circular patterns and designs, through which one could peep at the beck below, through which the light filtered, causing a lace-like effect, but through which the acrid stench never departed.

This odious place did a roaring trade. Within a few hundred yards radius were at least a couple of dozen pubs and clubs, and ale in those days was both strong and cheap.

I don't know for certain, but in retrospect it looks to me as if it must have drained straight into the beck.

This rat-infested, polluted mess, twisted and turned its sluggish way between the close-packed houses and cellar-dwellings of Damside, Pinfold and Greengate, on its way to join the River Worth, and so on to the River Aire at Stockbridge.

SLAP-BANG in the middle of this lot was the slaughter-house, screened at one side by the gas-tarred, but rotten wooden cattle sheds and "starving-'oles," and at the other by a high dry-stone wall, easily climbed by nosey kids on their way to and from the first of the important places mentioned at the start of this story.

This was an establishment known far and wide as "Ike Emmott's Wholesale and Retail Fruit and Vegetable Merchants." Here we could buy for twopence, one large paper carrier-bag, resplendent on the outside with the vendor's name, calling and address, and a picture in natural colours of a wicker-work basket, overflowing with apples, oranges, bananas, plums, pears, peaches, grapes (blue and green), cherries etc., etc., but filled with one kind of fruit only: "Two pennorth of loose bananas please!"

All the over-ripe, squashed and mis-shapen throw-outs they were; enough to feed six "hungry-faced" kids for a week, despite the half-dozen or so devoured before home was reached. A "God-send" indeed.

On to the next of our places of "God's gifts to the poor and needy!"

From "Ike" Emmott's in High Street, turn along the side of the old "Ship Inn," (since demolished) towards what is now the West Yorkshire Bus Company's garage and there under the "Chinese Club," (real name, "The Warehouseman's Club") and now Tony Kildunne's Betting Shop, was situated a famous place indeed — Soutar's Bakery. Within this worthy place, one could for the sum of one penny — I repeat, one humble "clod" — buy a huge paper bag, or if one was crafty enough to take a paper "carrier" (and you can bet your Father's best booits, we were crafty enough), full to the top with broken Vanilla slices (one's mouth waters to this very day at the thought of it), stale buns, coconut macaroons, almond tarts, jam tarts and lemon cheese tarts.

The icing and the glace cherries on these were as hard as the cast-iron surrounding that — but let us not mention such things in the same sentence.

Our eager teeth were a durn-sight harder. Dare one say it, amonst such dubious surroundings: "Manna from Heaven!"

I SUPPOSE now I've reached the bit where I've got to tell you what we saw over that wall. It makes me feel sick to have to describe it. It'll make you feel sick if you read it, but I know, by the same compulsion which made us heave our reluctant bodies to the top of that wall, you'll read it alright.

So don't say I didn't warn you.

From out of one of them sleazy-looking, rotten wooden sheds, screaming and bellowing, kicking and struggling, its eyes wide open and blood-shot with fear, was dragged the terrified victim.

There was a rope around its neck, twisted round one of its horns, down through two iron rings in the stone-cobbled yard, and in to the hands of a brawny-armed slaughter-man's mate who, with mighty heaves dragged the unfortunate creature's head down on to the cobble-stones.

The slaughter-man raised his pole-axe, an evil looking weapon with a chopper at one side of the stout wooden shaft, and a countersunk, sharpened round metal tube on the other.

Our stomachs turned over; our mouths went dry; sweat poured from our brows; and our hearts pounded twenty to the dozen. Still, somehow we couldn't jump down off that wall.

Up and back went the pole-axe, hung a second in mid-air whilst the "executioner" took aim, then down it came with a terrific "clunk," the object being to make a neat round hole dead centre in the beast's skull through which a thin stick called a "pith-cane" could be pushed to stir up the brains.

Blood and excrement flew in all directions. The noise was terrible. The other cattle awaiting their turn to die sensed what was happening. They bellowed, they howled. They tugged at their ropes and chains in an attempt to escape. All in vain.

On occasions the slaughter-man missed his mark, often once, many times twice, sometimes three times .. we jumped down from the wall, green as grass. The contents of our greedily-filled stomachs splashed over the ground, loose bananas, Vanilla slices, stale jam-tarts, the lot.

That same night I'd wake up in bed trembling and sweating from a fearful dream.

The rope was round my neck. I kicked. I struggled. I was being dragged down towards those iron rings . . .

THE GASLAMP

FOCAL point of the village. Especially on winter's nights.

You can climb up it.

Swing upside down on it.

Chalk your cricket wickets on it.

Tie your enemies to it.

You can light your tar-band off it and later on when nobody's watching you can light your tab-ends off it.

Besides all this it gives light for playing cig.-cards against the wall and marbles and piggy and stick and kick-can in the road.

Hmm! — useful things, Gaslamps.

FRIDAY NIGHT

INTO the tub, two at a time, (don't touch the side of the bath nearest the fire, it's hot).

A good doing over with red carbolic, out on to the tab-rug, dried, head protected from "wild-life" with paraffin, blood purified with a generous spoonful of brimstone and treacle — Ugh! Coughs and colds attended to with Veno's Cough Mixture, "lungs greased" with goose-grease spread thickly on brown paper applied to the chest, bowels regulated with Cascara tablets.

"Good-night — God bless" . . . and so to bed stinking like a poke of devils.

The Scissor Grinder

OLD MOTHBALLS

"OLD MOTHBALLS" was another one of Keighley's many, many "characters."

A friend of mine whose father used to keep a well-known pub in Keighley, told me "Old Mothballs'" real name was Albert Fearnley.

He came from a well-known family of manufacturing chemists over Heckmondwike way.

Perhaps this was the source of supply of his stock-in-trade, and, of course, the origin of his nick-name.

He would often call in at the aforesaid pub and ask the landlord to give him racing tips, written on a piece of old cardboard, or chalked on his battered old bowler hat. This, along with the sale of mothballs, was part of his daily "service" to the long-suffering but ever-tolerant public of Keighley in the 1920's and 30's.

You see it is an offence to beg in the streets, but the sale of mothballs and racing tips made him an "Itinerant Salesman," thus, out of reach of the "long arm of the law."

I'm afraid the tips weren't always very reliable, oft times being figments of my friend's dad's humorous imagination. The one shown in the picture, for instance, "*Water-Tap*." When this one was written down for him, "Old Mothballs" enquired, "Is it the Favourite?" to which the reply was: "No, but it's a damn good runner!"

He was a likeable old boy, and would always give "us kids" a few of his strong-smelling wares. What we did with them I can't for the life of me think.

The following story has nothing whatever to do with "Old Mothballs," but writing the last paragraph reminded me of it. My Dad used to say: "By Gow, if we'd some ham, we'd have ham and eggs for tea if nobbut we had some eggs!"

Just one more little story now, and then you'll have to move on.

"Old Mothballs" stood at the bar of this 'ere pub one day, laughing and joking with the customers. One of them had to go out to the "Gents," leaving his nearly full pint on the bar. As soon as he was out of sight, our "not-so-daft" hero dropped a mothball in to the unguarded glass. On returning, the man took one sip from his pint, spluttered it out all over the floor, gasping "Hell, I can't sup that b———r!"

Without hesitation, "Old Mothballs" picked up the the glass and said "Tha's reight lad, I'll sup it for thee; and downed the lot.

CHICKEN BROTH DAYS

THE HARKER'S had six fine sons and one daughter. Mrs. Harker was a big, jolly, kind-hearted woman. On Chicken-Broth days we'd all be there, six Harker lads, three Boardmans, "Broggy" Bryden, Billy Ward, the lot.

She used to say: "When tha's seven kids of thi' own, two or three more dooant mak mich difference!"

We were all supplied with a dish and a spoon, the big black iron pot full of delicious, bubbling broth was stood on a newspaper in the middle of the spotlessly-scrubbed whitewood table, then it was "ivvery man for 'isself!"

Our kindly hostess stood back and laughed and laughed 'til the tears rolled down her rosy cheeks.

Chicken-Broth is still one of my favourite dishes, but it never seems to have quite the flavour it had when we all stood around the Harker table like a lot of little pigs around a trough, whilst the long-gone Mrs. Harker stood back and laughed, and laughed, and laughed.

TICKLING TROUT

WE USED to crack that old gag: "My brother and I can answer any question on any subject under the sun. Ask us anything you like and my brother and I will give you the answer.

On being asked a question the reply was always the same: "Oh!, that's one of the things my brother knows, and he's not here to-day!"

But when it came to tickling trout, that was one thing brother Ron really did know. He was an expret.

Out of the house, up to the top of the lane to t'wood snicket, down the first field with the Hawthorn bush by the side of the path where we would have a snack of "Bread and Cheese" (Hawthorn leaves and the brownish red berries). I must confess, they never tasted like "Bread and Cheese" to me, but if brother Ron could eat them, then so could I.

Through the second snicket and down the stepping stones, a short stop for a drink of the icy-cold water from the old stone well, and so down the hill to the beck. Over "Tinker Bridge," along the path through the mushroom field, the one with the white horse in it ("Good luck to thee, good luck to me, good luck to every white horse I see"), and so on to the "Buttercliffe," a beautiful rock-strewn stream with deep, shady pools, beneath the overhanging trees.

Down on to his tummy on the bank, the sleeves of his shabby old jersey rolled high up his thin strong arms, slowly but surely his hand would slip in to the cold water, feeling gently under the mossy stones — the only sound the bubbling and gurgling as the peaty brown water tumbled over the rocks on its way to the beck.

Steady — steady — not a murmur — steady — easy does it — easy — easy — then . . . splash — whoosh . . . with a deft flick of his fingers, out on to the opposite bank where I was waiting would land, wriggling and squirming, a beautiful, big, fat, brown trout.

OLD BILL CROW

OLD BILL was a blacksmith's striker. He worked long hard hours and when he came home at night, he was black from the top of his cap to the bottom of his big bull clogs.

On Sundays he got dressed up. Cap, tie, suit, socks and big shiny boots were all as black as coal. You see, Bill never went out of mourning for his first wife who had her fourth child, and then just wasted away.

That's the reason "us kids" christened him "Old Bill Crow."

We used to pull his leg about this, (kids can be very cruel). We'd say to him, " 'Ow are ya Bill?" and before we could go any further he'd reply, "No better for thee askin,' and one day tha'll laike wi' t'bull 'til tha gets t'horns up thi . . . . . (behind)."

Then one sad day, just like everybody else seems to do, poor old "Bill Crow" died.

As his coffin was being slid in to the magnificent horse-drawn hearse, a neighbour was heard to remark, " 'E's bin shoein' 'osses for donkey's years, an' this is t'first time 'e's ivver 'ad a ride in a carriage. By gow! this must be t'poshest day of Old Bill's life."

LIVIN' OWER T'BRUSH

"BY GOW, LIZZIE, es ta eeard abaht yon ats cum ta live i' t'owd cottage next to t'wood snicket ?"

"Naw lass, goo on, tell ma, whattivvers ta dew wi' 'em ?"

"Well, tha knaws ahm nut one as likes ta talk abaht fowkses bizness . . . mich . . ."

"Gerron wi' it do, let's be knawin', what ev the' dun ?"

"Well, ah'll tell tha, dusta knaw, it's all ower t'loin, ther nut wed . . .!"

"Eeeeeeeeee, tha nivver sez!"

"That's weer tha't wrang, that's just what ah dew say, 'cos Maggie Murgitroyd telled me, an' if shew sez soa, tha can bet thi best booits it's reight, shew's nivver wrang, yon!"

"By 'eck, ah'll go tuv our 'ouse. Did ta ivver 'ear t'likes of it, the brazzen cheek on it . . . whativver's t'world cummin' tew, livin' ower t'brush, well ah reckon that's laatest . . . Eeeeeeeeee!"

CLOCKWORK TRAIN SETS

NOW, seeing as some fifty odd years have passed, I think the time is appropriate to convey my gratitude, without embarrassing anybody unduly, to a certain well-known firm of Keighley Ironmongers, for the important part they played in the Christmasses of of our boyhood.

This they did quite unwittingly, and I'm afraid, without a penny piece profit to their worthy selves.

In the 1920's, the business of this still-thriving family concern, was carried on in a double-windowed shop in Church Green.

Two or three weeks before Christmas, we watched those windows eagerly, until there appeared as if by magic, a beautiful yellow poster, announcing, in red and blue letters, *"Hornby Clockwork Train Sets for Christmas."*

In place of the usual hammers, saws, nails, screwdrivers, and the endless array of items peculiar to Ironmongers, stood the most fascinating display you ever did see.

Set out in the middle of the floor of the window, was a terrific "figure-eight" lay-out of train lines. On these lines were the most delightful objects ever made by the hand of man.

There were Red Engines, Blue Engines, Green Engines, Pullman Coaches, Coal Tenders, Goods Trucks, and Guards' Vans.

Along the back of the window was a red-roofed white-tiled Station-House, made of tin, standing on a Platform, with real railings, and signs and advertisements saying *"Bovril Prevents That Sinking Feeling." "Robin Starch." "Atora Beef Suet"* and the like.

There were little lead seats, with little lead people sitting on them. There was a whole little lead family, Mum, Dad, little girl and little boy, all with little lead suitcases, and even a little lead dog on a little lead lead, all waiting for the train to come along and take them on their holidays.

Obviously, rich little lead people.

There were little lead porters, wheeling little lead barrows, full of little lead portmanteaux, and a little lead Station-Master with a little green flag, and a whistle in his little lead mouth.

There were two little lead men walking across the window with a long lead plank on their shoulders bearing the legend *"Hall's Distemper."*

We looked, and we looked, and we looked. After school the following evening, we looked and we looked, and we looked again and on every following evening right up 'till Christmas Eve we looked and we looked and we looked and we looked.

The next Christmas we looked again, and the Christmas after that, again we looked, and we looked, and we looked.

Eventually, we grew too old, and stopped looking.

To this very day, I can still feel the magic of those wonderful displays of *"Hornby Clockwork Train Sets."*

Whilst we were pressing our noses longingly against the window, there was a young man inside the shop serving his apprenticeship as an Ironmonger. The same, not-quite-so-young man still works for the same firm. He told me the other day, we could have been the oh, so proud owners of one of the more humble train sets — No. 01 I think he said — for about twelve shillings.

But, consider this, there were five other children besides myself in our family. Had Mum have bought us each a Christmas present costing 12s. that would have come to £3-12-0. Dad's 38s. per week as a paper-maker at Turkey Mills, Goose-Eye, just didn't run to gifts of such grandeur.

We looked at them as people look at the Crown Jewels in the Tower of London (or wherever it is they keep them), admiring them, savouring their sheer beauty, but never coveting them, knowing that they were beyond the reach of ordinary mortals like you and me.

LET us now move on fifty years.

I had decided to record in paint, the happy things, the sad things, all the things I remember of our boyhood in the 1920's.

Just up Tower Hill at Steeton, a few doors above the old barn I use as a studio, there lives a gentleman, retired some three or four years ago, from the

"Tha'll lewk after it
weeant ta lad . . ."

Bobbin-Mill, where he had worked since he was a boy.

Most mornings he goes for a walk. Often he calls to see how I'm "getting on wi t'Exhibition." He is "varry interested." The picture he seemed to show most interest in was the one of my ginger mate and I worshipping at the shrine of the aforesaid ironmongers' window.

He isn't a man who "wears his heart on his sleeve " but eventually he announced most solemnly one day: "I'm bahn ta tell tha summat nah lad. Tha sees yon pickter theer wi' them train sets on it. Well, I've nivver said nowt abaht it to onnybody afore, but I did just same thing as thee, at yon same shop window, a year or two afore tha wor old enniff, and I'll tell thi summat else nah, I nivver got one awther. This efternooin, I'm coming back, an' I'll show tha summat as'll cap tha."

Sure enough, after dinner, back came my friend, with a parcel under his arm.

"Nah then lad" he began, "I've browt this ere, and I'm bahn ta give it to thee to put wi' yon pickter in thi Exhibition in't Castle.

Tha sees, when I grew up an' gat wed, I hed a son o' me own, an' as sooin as 'e wor owd enniff, I I went to yon shop an' bowt this 'ere Clockwark Train Set for 'im. He played with it for years an' years 'till 'e grew aht on it. Then it wor mine.

"Well, lad, nobody knows owt abaht it nobbut thee an' me, but I've 'ed it 'idden ivver since. Nah I've decided tha's gettin on for sixty I think it's time tha hed one for thisself, so I'm bahn ta gi' tha it!"

He put the parcel in my hand, turned quickly round and went down the old wooden steps.

Half way down he hesitated, and without looking back, said, "Tha'll lewk after it weeant ta lad . . ."

The Rentman

STREET GAMES

S. R. BOARDMAN

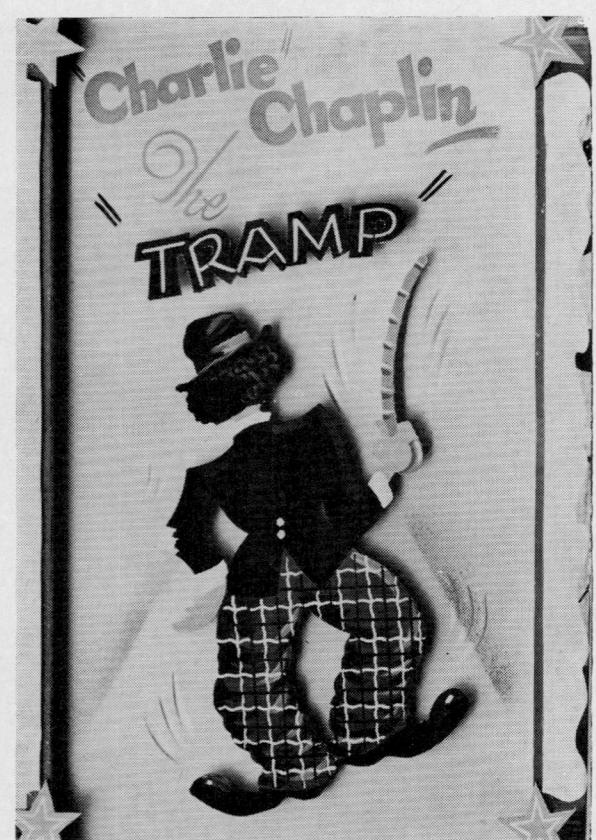

IT'S SATURDAY!

YIPPEE! . . . no school . . . the happiest day of the week.

Up in the morning and away.

A few coppers to be earned running errands for the neighbours.

A quick dash down to the bottom of t'lane for a pound and a half of Hird's renowned sausages.

My favourite dinner, sausage and mash, even though the sausages always tasted too peppery.

Queue up for the "Saturday Penny" from Dad.

A good wash . . . "No cat-licks now, wash behind them ears!"

Out with the Cherry Blossom boot polish (the smell of this reminds me of Saturday dinner-time to this very day. I think it must have been the only time we cleaned 'em.)

Clogs brushed: "Hey, our Stan, you haven't cleaned the backs!"

Then . . . Ya-hoo! . . . off like the clappers to Fell Lane bottom, a pennorth of Gob-stoppers, (4 a 1d.), in to the queue for "The Oxy-'all" picture-house.

A pennorth in "The Planks, please!" (the wooden forms in the front few rows).

A shouting, fighting, laughing, Gob-stopper sucking crowd of the happiest kids in the world.

SATURDAYS ... Going In ...

SATURDAYS . . . Coming Out . . .

PIGGY AND STICK

I'VE HEARD it called "*Billet and Stick* —

"*Tip-Cat*" — "*Buck and Stick*" and various other names not fit to be repeated in a salubrial place like this, when an extra good swipe has sent the "Piggy" straight through a window.

An Italian hairdresser who came to see me about a sign, told me he used to play the same game (with slight variations) when he was a boy in Italy. His name for it, "*Mazza E Piusola*."

My niece, a schoolteacher in Bolton, told me they had a lot of Asian children at her school and she often sees them playing it in the school yard.

She said she would ask them what they called it and that she would write and let me know.

She forgot.

I have a friend whose sister married a handsome Pakistani man. She said she would ask her sister if she would ask her husband.

She did.

He said they call it, "*Guli-Danda-Dunda*."

Isn't that super? I like that name best of all.

FREDDY GRAMOPHONE

HIS old gramophone wasn't worth tuppence.

I suppose it would fetch quite a few quid now as an antique.

The noise the records made was only outrivalled in unintelligibility by Freddy's own raucous voice.

It sounded as if he was giving everybody a good cussing for the smallness of lack or contributions dropped into his greasy old cap, which was used for collecting purposes only, I never saw him wearing it.

In later years, he mustn't have done too badly, the decrepit old pram was scrapped, it's place being taken by quite a reasonable, joiner-made cart.

One of the greatest "bug-bears" of his life was in the person of one John Thomas Bradley.

"John Thomas" was equally as "famous" as Freddy Gramophone in those days. His real vocation was that of "Itinerant Firewood Merchant."

His "outfit" wasn't in the same class as Freddy's — a mere soap-box on two tired, but tyreless pram wheels minus several spokes, with two butter-tub lathes for shafts.

In summer when the firewood trade dropped dead, John Thomas would bring out a little old portable gramophone without a horn, load it on to his soap-box, and head for the theatre queue.

Now everybody in the world knew, the theatre queue had belonged to Freddy Gramophone ever since gramophones had been invented.

A sheer, blatant act of violation of human rights. There was 'ell on.

Without any hesitation Freddy would go into action. He'd froth and foam at the mouth. He'd wave his arms about. He'd make bold rushes in John Thomas's direction, threatening and fuming.

I once saw him take a wild kick at John Thomas's "outfiit", miss, and land up in a heap of old rags on the ground.

Believe you me, you didn't need "wirelesses" or "tellys" in those days.

There used to be some magnificent shows at the old Keighley Hippodrome, but the theatregoers often had as many laughs outside the theatre for a copper or two, as they did inside for two or three bob.

SMITH HARKER, THREE-HORSE MAN

THERE are many theories as to how the massive blocks of stone were transported to build the pyramids of Egypt, but the methods used will never be known for certain.

In case anyone 1973 years or so from now would like to know how . . . in the 1920's, Smith Harker moved ten ton blocks of stone from Barret's Branshaw Quarries, Oakworth, up Stell Hill and down Fell Lane to the stone yard in Keighley, there to be sawn into slabs for gravestones or various sizes for building purposes. I have spent many instructive and amusing hours talking to Smith, now 83 years of age, still fit enough to be able to walk five or six miles on the same old road every day, in an effort to put his feats on record.

Smith Harker was a "three-horse man." He arose every morning around about four o'clock and walked the couple or so miles from his home in Fell Lane to the quarries owned by the Barret family at Branshaw, Oakworth. He started work at 5.45 a.m.

The fact that he was a *three*-horse man entitled him to 4s. more than the other quarry men, bringing his wage up to the grand total of 24s. per week; but bear in mind, even though the quarry wasn't worked on Sundays, Smith still had to go to feed and water his horses, groom them until they shone like silk, "muck out" the stable, dubbin the harness, and polish the horse brasses . . .

In those days money wasn't the only consideration, a man was proud of his "turn-out."

After being hacked from the quarry face, the huge blocks of stone were lifted by steam crane on to Smith's low three tons flat wagon. The squat wheels had eight-inch wide iron "tyres" and hefty wooden-blocked brakes. The three Shire horses, "Captain", "Dick" and "Dolly" were yoked into the shafts.

"Giddup there!" with a terrific lunge forward the powerful animals started on their long haul.

The first mile was comparitively easy, flat going.

With a rythmic clip-clop, clip-clop of hooves, the creaking of the heavily-laden cart and an occasional encouraging "go on Captain!" . . . "Get on there, Dick!" . . . "Steady Dolly!" from Smith they reached the foot of the steep Stell Hill.

From here on I think it would be clearer if the following diagrams take up the story.

Off we go again.

The brakes full on, Captain, Dick and Dolly, straining back on the breeching straps with all their might, from the top of Stell Hill the road falls steeply into Fell Lane, past Harry Moore's farm. Steeper still to Holme House Wood snicket. Pressure of the wooden brake blocks against the iron rims emitting alternate squeels and groans like some mighty yodeller, able to be heard by "us kids" on our reluctant way to Holycroft School, as far away as t'bottom of t'lane almost a mile away.

On reaching "Bobby Lane" which leads to Stell's tube mill, the road mercifully levels off and Smith could temporarily relax.

After stopping to release the brakes, two or three buckets of water were thrown over the hot smoking brake blocks. A short rest to cool off and so on to Keighley.

This happened two or three times every day, summer and winter. On occasions in very wet weather, Smith would call at his cottage half way between the quarries and Keighley to change his wringing wet clothes, sometimes twice, sometimes thrice. But as he says, "that wor all part of t'job."

ONE of the many amusing stories Smith told me concerned his mate "Pick" Inman, who assisted with braking etc. over Stell Hill (a bit of a character). "Pick" (short for Pickard) was walking to work early one morning when he had to bend down to fasten his leather boot lace. As he did so the pint bottle of cold tea he always carried fell out of his inside jacket pocket and smashed on the road.

On answering a knock on the cottage door Smith's wife Elsie was confronted by "Pick" who enquired: "Is Smith in?"

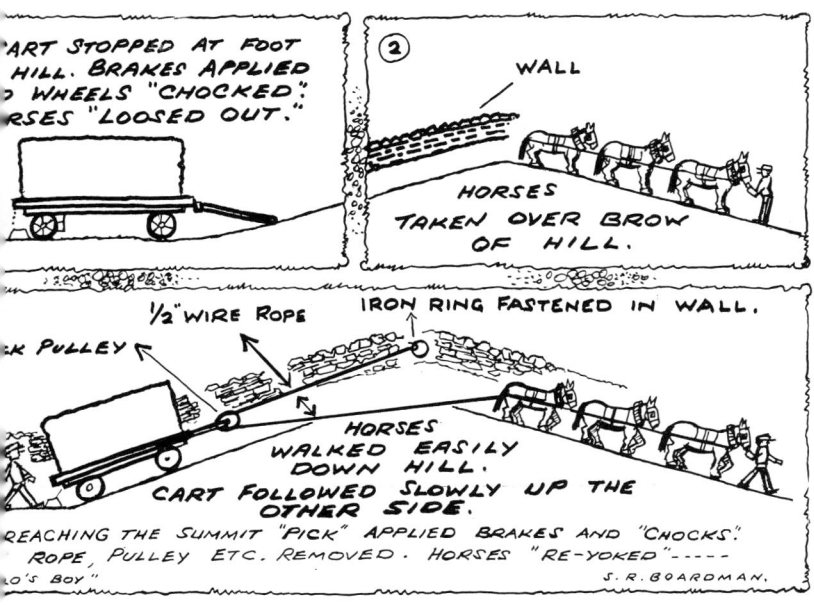

"No, he's gone to his wark!"

"Well, I'm sorry to trouble thi lass, but 'ast tha got a bottle to fit this ere cork, an' if tha' 'as does ta think tha' could find a drop of teea to put in it?"

Another one was about one of his neighbours "old Ned Scott." Old Ned told some of the Fell Lane kids that his bike had "hed young uns." If they wanted a young bike they could have one if they brought a blanket to wrap it up in, so "it didn't catch it's deeath o'cold!"

On presenting themselves hopefully at Ned's door complete with blankets, two of the lads were told: "By gum, tha can't hev one just now, it's upstairs feeding 'em and if I go onny where near it, it'll kick me tot'deeath!"

Having painted the picture and written the story of Smith Harker and his beloved horses, I showed them to him for his approval (or otherwise). He was very pleased but said "I must admit when tha first came asking all them questions I couldn't see what all t'fuss wor abaat. I didn't think I'd owt out of t'ordinary to tell thee!"

KEIGHLEY TARN

BEFORE the First World War there lived on a farm called High Redcar on the hills overlooking Keighley Tarn a young man by the name of Frank Taylor.

He used to look down on to the peaceful stretch of water and dream a dream.

Before that dream could be fulfilled young Frank had to go and fight in the ghastliest bloody war of all time.

He joined the Dublin Fusiliers and was wounded in one of the terrible battles in France.

After several weeks in a Military Hospital in England he made a good recovery and was due to return to the fighting.

Whilst in Dover, awaiting a troopship to carry him and his companions across the channel, a Destroyer limped in to port with three great holes rent in its side.

On making enquiries Frank was told that the holes were made by German torpedoes.

The thing that struck him most, being of an engineering and mechanical turn of mind, was the thin gauge of metal used to build the ship.

This observation he stored away in his mind for future reference.

In 1919 Frank Taylor was demobbed from the army and returned to Keighley to find that the people who owned the farm he had lived on before the war had decided they wanted it for themselves and that he could no longer live there.

On the bank of the Tarn stood a stone building, the property of Keighley Ice Skating Club. This had been built to replace their two previous wooden club houses that had been destroyed by fire.

Having nowhere to live, the by now, married Frank approached the secretary of the Skating Club and asked if he could live in the Club House and become Curator and Keeper of the Tarn.

Agreement was reached.

He could rent the property for the sum of 4s. per week with added conditions.

These were that he looked after the ice in winter, keeping it in good smooth condition for skating (a very popular winter pastime in the 1920's and 30's).

This he did by spraying the surface of the ice every night with an old hand operated Fire-Engine water pump.

Frank Taylor during the First World War.

Besides this he had to keep a stock of sweets, chocolates, cigarettes etc., and make cups of tea and snacks.

In return for these duties Frank was allowed to use the Tarn for boating in the summer months.

RECALLING the thin sheet metal used to build the Destroyer he had seen in Dover Harbour, he devised a method of making his own canoes and rowing boats.

If you go up to Keighley Tarn today, walk across to the far bank and look in to the corner on your right you will see three boat-shaped concrete moulds set in the ground.

These have lain buried for years and years.

A team of lads plus one brave little lassie from South Craven School at Crosshills have spent several very strenuous days digging the earth away so you can see them.

Don't let them have toiled so gamely in vain; go up there and have a look for yourselves (there's a heck of a lot of fresh air up there and it will put some roses in your cheeks).

These moulds were the bottom half of a simple press.

The other half was in the form of a scrap-iron filled concrete boat shape weighing over five tons. This was suspended from a beam and was raised and lowered by hand operated Block and Tackle. (*See model*).

It took six sheets of metal 3′ 6″ x 4′ at 6s. per sheet to make one canoe.

The metal sheets were placed in to the bottom half of the mould and the heavy boat-shaped top half lowered on to them pressing them in to shape. The whole was then welded together to form the hull of the canoe.

When completed these were hired out by the hour.

I forget the exact price charged but remember if we walked up to the Tarn and told Frank we only had twopence, if it was fairly quiet he would let us stay out in a canoe all afternoon for that amount.

A great treat indeed. (Thank you, Frank.)

He also made canoes, painted them in bright colours, advertised them in a national Trade Magazine and got orders from all over the country.

Prices ranged from £5 for a small canoe up to £15 for the bigger boats.

On completion these were wheeled down to Keighley Station on an old pram for delivery by rail to his customers all over England.

This was all done at nights and week-ends; during the day he worked as a welder at the engineering works of Prince Smith's in Keighley.

Frank Taylor is still alive and 87 years of age.

He told me that after 16 years of this extremely hard life he left the cold, bleak windswept banks of Keighley Tarn and moved lower down Blackhill.

Despite all his ingenuity, his skill, his hard work and determination, Frank told me — rather sadly, — "In all them rough years I made nowt. I just managed to scrape a decent living for me and my family."

A model of Frank Taylor's boat-building mould.

Balloons for Rags

TURKEY MILLS STEAM WAGON

SPUD MICK

"SPUD MICK" and his "Tatie" engine stood against the goods yard railings at the bottom of Cavendish Street, Keighley, for donkey's years.

You could see your face in the brightly-polished metal and brass work of his roasted potato machine.

His boots were shiny and his apron "spotless."

But above all, the aroma — the flavour — the warmth of a coppersworth of piping hot "spuds" on a cold winter's day . . . !

"Spud Mick" has gone.

The railings and the goods yard are still there.

Just up the street there are posh cafes and restaurants and snack bars.

You can buy Kentucky Fried Chicken and Chips.

Scampi and Chips.

All the delicacies of the East in the Chinese Restaurants.

Continental food, Indian food, the lot!

None of them can compare for sheer enjoyment with the memory of the first careful, mouth-watering bite in to one of "Spud Mick's" humble "Hot Roasted Potatoes."

Playing at Oxo (Look at their legs)

THE PAWNBROKERS

FOR THE uninitiated, perhaps I'd better give a brief explanation of "Pawnshop procedure," or "Popping," as we called it, at the "Pop-shop."

Quite simply, the pawnbroker was a money lender. One borrowed money from him, using whatever valuables one possessed, as security.

Every Monday morning there would be a queue a "mile long," mostly women, each with a brown paper parcel under her arm, containing her husband's "best suit," to be "popped" until Friday (pay-day) for 10s. or a £1, depending on the condition and quality of the garments (less a few coppers — "Ticket-Brass").

Come Friday, one would have to pay back the amount borrowed, plus a shilling or two interest, to retrieve the "old-man's" suit, ready for the week-end.

My mother used to say to me: "Have a good look round Stan. If you see anyone you know, walk straight past, then go back again when they've gone!" She was a very proud sort of a woman, and felt ashamed of having to pawn our vests etc., to get a few bobs with which to buy food.

I didn't learn this until many years later, but she had already sent one of my brothers a few days earlier with her wedding ring. She had a cheap brass one to wear, whilst her gold one was in "pop," so that the neighbours wouldn't notice it was missing.

My instructions were to ask for 2s. for the half-dozen vests. Not the very best quality vests I fear, and not in the very best of condition either, having had a long, hard life, with many boilings in the "copper," many "possings" in the "peggy-tub."

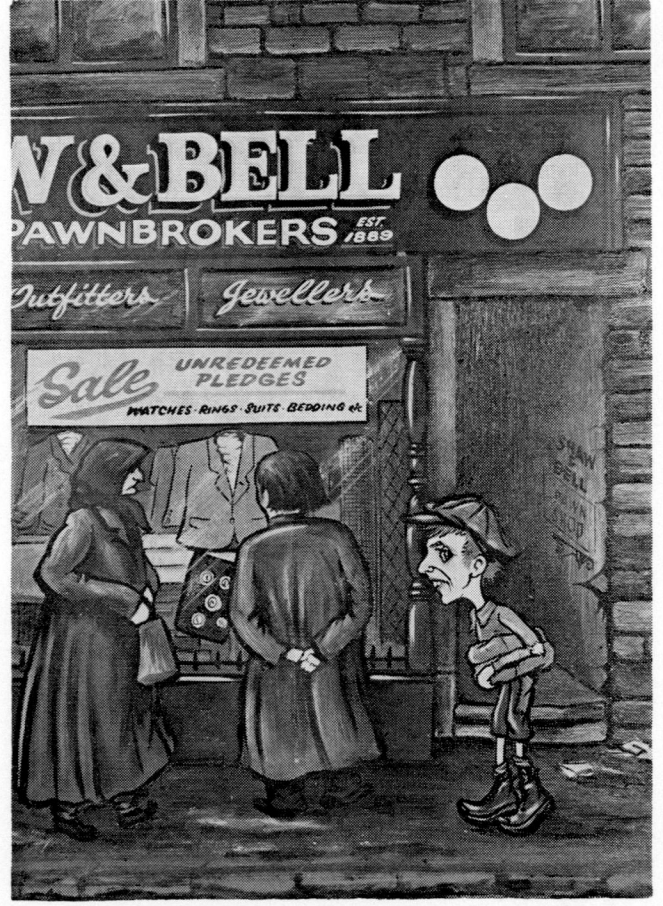

and many scrubbings on the rubbing-board. At least, they were always "spotless clean," if nothing else.

Nine times out of ten, I'd fall short of the desired target of 2s. "They're full of holes" the man behind the counter used to say." "They're worth nowt really, but tha' looks pined to t'deeath, and fair nithered; here lad, take this eighteen-pence, and off tha' gooas hooam!"

If, at the end of twelve months one didn't retrieve one's vests, suits, watches, clocks, bedding or whatever one had pawned, they became the property of the pawnbroker. He then sold them for a profit as "Unredeemed Pledges."

I often wondered . . . What the 'ell he would have done with our shabby old vests if we hadn't gone back for them?

One Monday morning, a woman walked in to the Pawnshop with a square, heavy looking brown paper parcel, put it on the counter, and said "How mich?"

The assistant untied the string, took off the paper to reveal a handsome black marble clock (very fashionable in the 1920's).

"I'll give you £1." "Right" said the woman, took the £1 (less a few coppers "Ticket Brass") and went on her way).

The following Friday evening she came back, paid her £1 (plus the pawnbroker's interest), collected the clock, and left.

Monday morning, back she came with the parcel, and the transaction was completed as before.

This went on week after week, until it became a regular routine. Monday, in; Friday, out. Monday, in; Friday, out. Same square, brown paper parcel, which had become so familiar, the assistant used to put it on the shelf without opening it.

Then one Friday the woman didn't come to redeem the parcel, and it stood on the shelf for twelve months.

When the time was up, the pawnbroker took down the parcel from the shelf, ready to value the clock and put it up for sale. He untied the string, rolled it up neatly and put it in the string box. Took off the brown paper wrapping, and there stood on the counter, as handsome a pair of red bricks as you ever did see.

Gypsies

The Seaside Special

The Sandwich-Board Man

SUNSET

WHAT a day!

We've been down in t'wood digging pig-nuts.

We've had a swim in t'Tube Mill dam.

We've pinched one of Albert Emmott's turnips and had blackberries for afters.

We've swung across t'stream up t'Buttercliffe on the overhanging branches and we've slid down t'bank on our britches behinds.

Then we crossed t'fields and up on to Branshaw Moor, reight on up past Newsholme Village, on to Slippery Ford.

We went reight ower to'moor to t'Big Dam and were going to have another swim but by heck that watter's too deng cold.

We had a cap full of bilberries for dinner washed down with icy peat-brown water from a moorland stream, as we listened to the grouse telling us to "Go-back, Go-back."

We've climbed to the top of Cowling Pinnacle and looked at that breath-taking view.

The Curlews were crying.

The Peewits were laughing as they practised victory rolls in the air, and the Skylarks dropped like stones out of the sky . . .

Now it's time to go home to bed just one last look at the sunset . . .

It hasn't cost us a penny.

It's a good job; we haven't got one anyway.